W9-ACW-074

CONQUERORS
& EXPLORERS

© Aladdin Books Ltd 1996

Designed and produced by
Aladdin Books Ltd
28 Percy Street
London W1P 0LD

*First published in
the United States in 1996 by*
Copper Beech Books,
an imprint of
The Millbrook Press
2 Old New Milford Road
Brookfield
Connecticut 06804

Editor
Jim Pipe
Design
David West Children's Books
Designer
Flick Killerby
Picture Research
Brooks Krikler Research
Illustrators
Francesca D'Ottavi, Alessandro Bartolozzi,
Lorenzo Cecchi, Susanna Addario, Claudia
Saraceni – McRae Books, Florence, Italy

Printed in Belgium

Library of Congress Cataloging-in-Publication Data

Ross, Stewart.
Conquerors and explorers / by Stewart Ross: illustrated by
McRae Books
p. cm. -- (Fact or fiction)
Includes index.
Summary: Examines the facts and myths surrounding the
explorations of Odysseus, Christopher Columbus, Neil
Armstrong, and others.
ISBN 0-7613-0532-7 (lib. bdg.). --
ISBN 0-7613-0509-2 (pbk.)
1. Explorers--Juvenile literature. [1. Explorers.] I. McRae
Books. II. Title. III. Series: Ross, Stewart. Fact or fiction.
G175.R68 1996   96-17157
910'.92--dc20   CIP AC

FACT *or* FICTION:

CONQUERORS
& EXPLORERS

Written by *Stewart Ross*
Illustrated by *McRae Books, Italy*

COPPER BEECH BOOKS
BROOKFIELD, CONNECTICUT

CONTENTS

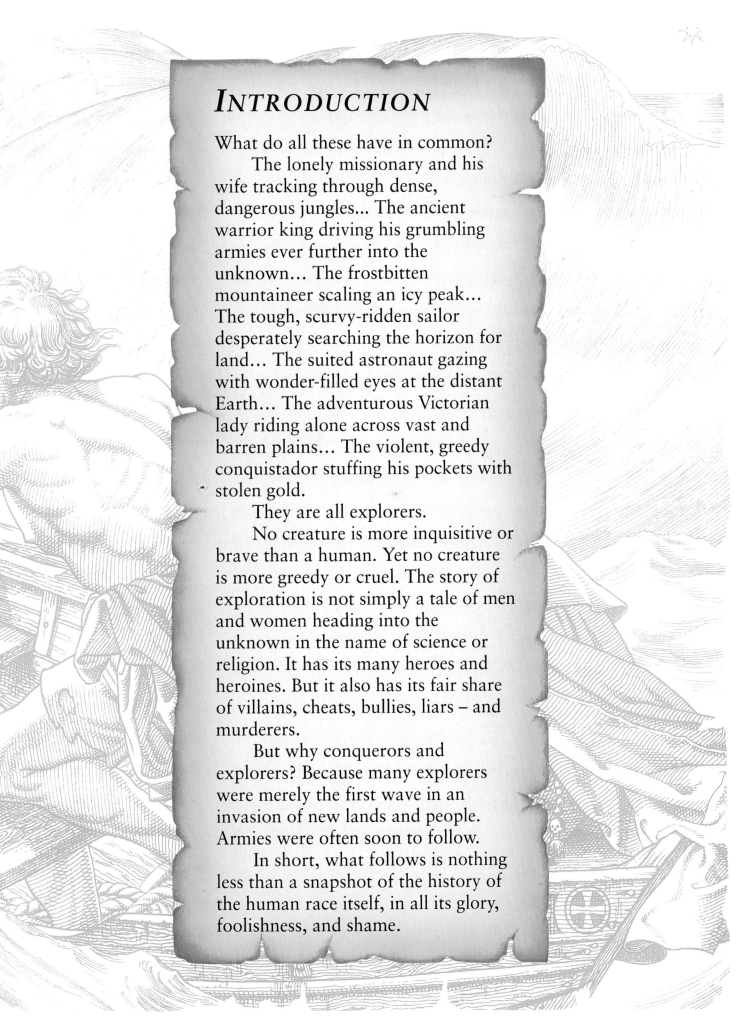

INTRODUCTION

What do all these have in common?

The lonely missionary and his wife tracking through dense, dangerous jungles... The ancient warrior king driving his grumbling armies ever further into the unknown... The frostbitten mountaineer scaling an icy peak... The tough, scurvy-ridden sailor desperately searching the horizon for land... The suited astronaut gazing with wonder-filled eyes at the distant Earth... The adventurous Victorian lady riding alone across vast and barren plains... The violent, greedy conquistador stuffing his pockets with stolen gold.

They are all explorers.

No creature is more inquisitive or brave than a human. Yet no creature is more greedy or cruel. The story of exploration is not simply a tale of men and women heading into the unknown in the name of science or religion. It has its many heroes and heroines. But it also has its fair share of villains, cheats, bullies, liars – and murderers.

But why conquerors and explorers? Because many explorers were merely the first wave in an invasion of new lands and people. Armies were often soon to follow.

In short, what follows is nothing less than a snapshot of the history of the human race itself, in all its glory, foolishness, and shame.

GOD, GREED, & ADVENTURE

Humans are travelers. Since their first appearance on the planet, they have explored unknown regions to piece together the jigsaw puzzle of the Earth and its solar system. A few explorers went where no human had ever been before – over uncharted oceans, across lifeless deserts, or out into space.

Some of these travelers marched at the head of armies, in search of new lands, treasures, and souls to conquer. Other bold adventurers simply longed to know what was over the horizon – but where they ventured, soldiers and missionaries were often sure to follow.

At the Edge of the World
Whatever else, explorers had guts. Some set sail still believing that they might be swept over the edge of the world (above).

Chinese Exploration by c.1500

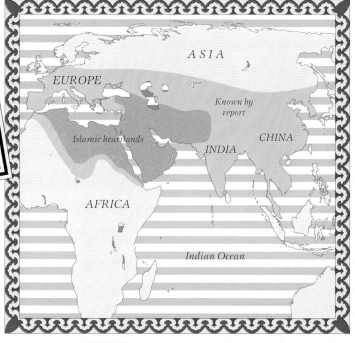

The Islamic World by c.1500 (above)

Self-Centered Civilizations (see maps)
In about 1200 A.D. the regions of the world were still cut off from each other. Each civilization thought it was at the center of the world. Before Western Europe's Age of Exploration, knowledge of other peoples and cultures was largely a collection of myths and distorted travelers' tales.

THE FIRST EXPLORERS?
Modern humans, sometimes known as *Homo sapiens*, emerged about 40,000 years ago. With the world still in the grip of the last Ice Age, these people lived in the warm regions around the equator.

As the ice sheet melted away, the first and greatest Age of Exploration began. As a result, by about 8000 B.C., humans could be found in almost every corner of the globe.

THE WORLD OF THE MAPMAKER

The history of exploration is also the history of the human view of the world. Old maps of the world can seem very confusing, because they were drawn according to religious ideals and traditional stories as much as from observation.

For example, Ptolemy's map (*right*), drawn in the 2nd century A.D. but used until the 15th century, shows a huge southern continent linking Africa and China. Not knowing its real shape ancient Buddhists drew the world in the shape of a Lotus flower.

WHY? – BECAUSE IT'S THERE...

Asked why he climbed Everest, a mountaineer replied: "Because it's there." Like him, many explorers went simply in search of adventure. Missionaries wanted to spread their religion among "unbelievers."

Others were driven by the thirst for wealth or power. Such brave but ruthless people were as much conquerors as explorers.

European Exploration by 1490 (above)

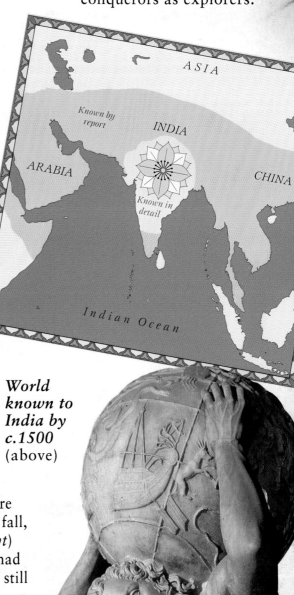

World known to India by c.1500 (above)

THE FRONTIERS OF KNOWLEDGE.

Fiction begins where knowledge ends. To explain why the sky did not fall, the ancient Greeks imagined the giant Atlas (*right*) carrying the sky on his shoulders. Even after Magellan had sailed right around the world in 1522, many Europeans still believed it was flat!

Early sailors believed that huge monsters dwelled over the horizon. Today we fill the region beyond our horizon – outer space – with equally weird and terrifying creatures, such as the deadly monster from the 1986 film *Aliens* (*left*).

INTO THE UNKNOWN

The young Greek prince wept at the news of his father's victory: "My father will conquer everything, and leave me nothing to do." But just twenty years later, the boy who became Alexander the Great (356–323 B.C.) had carved out an empire that stretched from the Adriatic Sea to India. In 326, he planned to go on to Ocean, the sea that ran around the very edge of the world. Exhausted and frightened, his army mutinied, and the greatest conqueror-explorer of all time was forced to turn back.

S IZE ISN'T EVERYTHING! In the 1956 film *Alexander the Great*, the lead role was played by a tall actor, Richard Burton (*above*). However, the film's makers had ignored the fact that the real king was only 4 ft 8 in!

Jason and the Argonauts (main picture)
On his way to steal the golden fleece, Jason steered his ship Argo *through the clashing Symplegades. He dashed between the rocks while they were rebounding from trying to crush the dove he had sent through earlier.*

EGYPTIAN TRAVELS

The first known explorer was the ancient Egyptian Harkhuf. In about 2300 B.C. the pharaoh sent him up the Nile to find the town of Yam in Nubia. Harkhuf returned with rare animals and a dancing dwarf. In 1970, Thor Heyerdahl sailed *Ra II* (*left*) across the Atlantic to prove the Egyptians could have done it 4,000 years ago.

THE GALLANT GREEK

Few ancient explorers were more daring than Pytheas, from the Greek colony of Marseilles. In about 308 B.C. he is said to have sailed out of the Mediterranean and north to England. Taking careful scientific measurements, he braved the supposed sea monsters and sailed around the British Isles to "Ultima Thule" – Norway or Iceland.

THE SILKEN THREAD

The oldest explorers' route winds across Asia from China to the Middle East. Known as the Silk Road, because of the West's passion for Oriental silks, it was pioneered by unknown merchants from the first century B.C. onward.

Merchant caravans, operating from bases such as Samarkhand and Khotan, conducted the trade in relays.

Easy Riders?

The Silk Road (the main routes are shown below) was no easy ride. In addition to the harsh desert landscape (above) there was the ever-present threat from murderous looters and bandits.

PERILS AT SEA?

The story of Jason and the clashing rocks is thought to refer to the entrance to the Black Sea, known today as the Dardanelles. Another theory is that *The Odyssey* is a coded navigation guide, with each of Odysseus's perils marking a real danger to ships.

THE JOURNEY HOME. Homer's epic Greek poem *The Odyssey* tells how Odysseus, a veteran from the siege of Troy, overcame many mythical perils on his ten-year journey home to Greece. Along the way Odysseus (shown *right* in the 1967 film *Ulysses*) battles against such terrors as the witch Circe, the one-eyed giant Polyphemus, and the twin terrors of Scylla and Charybdis (page 20).

TRAVELS IN THE ORIENT

"I am surprised," wrote the 15th-century Chinese interpreter Ma Huan, "that there are such differences in the world." His surprise rose to wonder when he traveled with Captain Cheng Ho (1404–1433) on his remarkable voyages of exploration. With 63 huge ships and 30,000 men, Cheng made seven voyages. He visited 30 countries between China and Africa (see map on page 22). On his seventh voyage, he sailed over 13,000 miles and returned home laden with exotic presents for the emperor – including an African giraffe (*main picture*)!

THE CENTRAL KINGDOM

Traditionally, the Chinese were not interested in exploration – China was at the center of the world (shown on this cosmic map, *left*), everywhere else was inferior, and therefore not worth bothering about! In map-making, however, they were centuries ahead of Europe.

Pointing the Way

In the third century A.D., *the Chinese pioneered the most effective piece of navigational equipment, the magnetic compass. To find north, European sailors relied on the stars* (left) *or a piece of magnetic rock known as a lodestone.*

TELL ME ANOTHER! Sinbad, who appears in the mythical stories of *Arabian Nights' Tales,* was also famous for his seven voyages. His adventures (*below*) were perhaps inspired by the tall tales of Arab sailors.

Junk Speed (below)
The huge oceangoing junks of Cheng Ho were said to have once covered 1,500 miles in only 14 days!

AN INCREDIBLE WHOPPER? In 1271, the 17-year-old Marco Polo (1254–1324) accompanied his father and uncle on an overland journey to the court of the great Kublai Khan, emperor of China (*top*).

Marco was amazed at what he saw. Chinese wealth and sophistication was unmatched anywhere in Christian Europe.

After serving the emperor for a while, in 1295 he sailed home. However, some scholars now believe much of his story may have been based on other travelers' tales – and that he went no further than the Middle East!

Mecca in the Middle
Islamic mapmakers borrowed heavily from the work of the ancient Greeks but placed their holy city, Mecca, at the center of their maps.

THE MEGA-MAP MAKER
The finest mapmaker of the medieval world was the Muslim traveler and scholar Abu Abdullah al-Idrisi (1099–1165). He drew a gigantic, 70-section world map for his Christian patron King Roger II of Sicily. Based on ancient Greek geography and his own observations, it was the first to suggest that there was no southern continent linking Africa to China (*above*).

THE GREAT SAGA

In 1000 A.D. Leif Ericson's Norwegian longship leaves Greenland and heads east. Soon a gale arises from the southeast. Leif is swept off course, northwest through heavy, cold seas.

When the gale subsides, Leif turns south to an unknown craggy shore, which he calls "Rockland." Further south, he discovers the more hospitable "Woodland" and "Vineland." Leif's epic voyage is all but forgotten. Hundreds of years later, when Europeans rediscover his western world, they rename it "America!"

Sun Seekers? (above)
The film Eric the Viking *highlighted the fact that the Vikings sailed south as well as west, even terrorizing towns along the North African coast.*

VINLAND HOAX?
Using a lost 14th-century original, in 1590 Sigurddar Stefansson drew the Viking's American discoveries on his "Vinland Map." Though the map is probably a fake, research suggests medieval Viking settlements existed as far west as the Missouri River.

Ships of the Atlantic (main picture)
The Viking ship, the knorr, *was long, narrow, and very seaworthy. Steered by an oar at the stern, it was driven by oars or a sail and could be easily hauled onto the beach. Later European explorers used carracks or caravels with the triangular Mediterranean sail.*

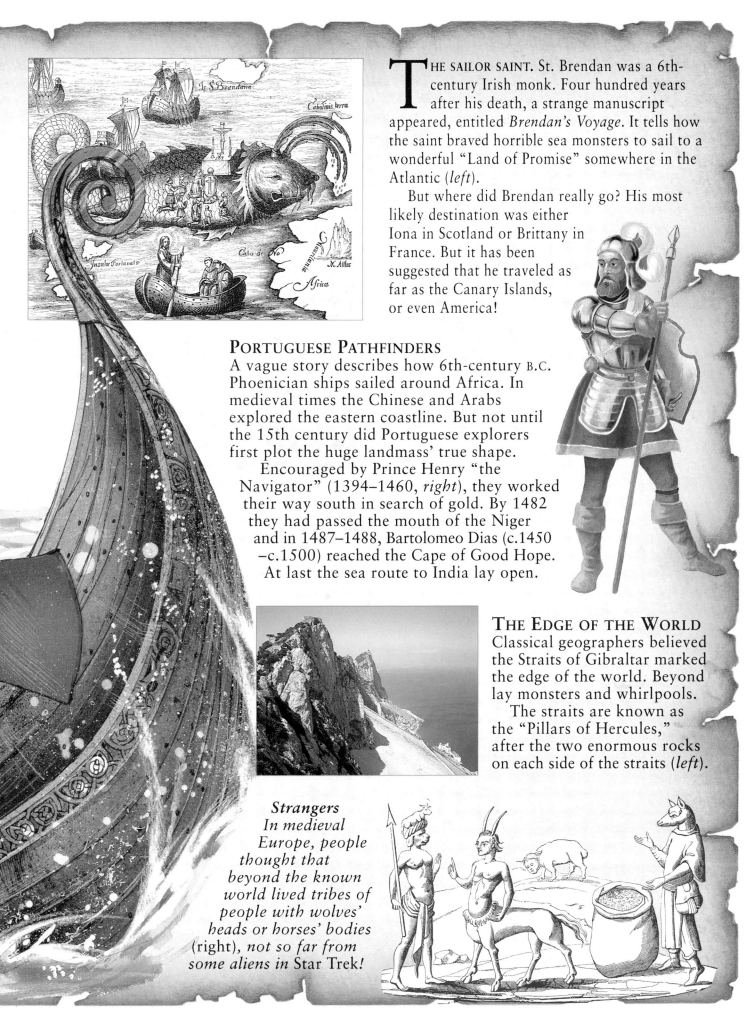

THE SAILOR SAINT. St. Brendan was a 6th-century Irish monk. Four hundred years after his death, a strange manuscript appeared, entitled *Brendan's Voyage*. It tells how the saint braved horrible sea monsters to sail to a wonderful "Land of Promise" somewhere in the Atlantic (*left*).

But where did Brendan really go? His most likely destination was either Iona in Scotland or Brittany in France. But it has been suggested that he traveled as far as the Canary Islands, or even America!

PORTUGUESE PATHFINDERS

A vague story describes how 6th-century B.C. Phoenician ships sailed around Africa. In medieval times the Chinese and Arabs explored the eastern coastline. But not until the 15th century did Portuguese explorers first plot the huge landmass' true shape.

Encouraged by Prince Henry "the Navigator" (1394–1460, *right*), they worked their way south in search of gold. By 1482 they had passed the mouth of the Niger and in 1487–1488, Bartolomeo Dias (c.1450 –c.1500) reached the Cape of Good Hope. At last the sea route to India lay open.

THE EDGE OF THE WORLD

Classical geographers believed the Straits of Gibraltar marked the edge of the world. Beyond lay monsters and whirlpools.

The straits are known as the "Pillars of Hercules," after the two enormous rocks on each side of the straits (*left*).

Strangers
In medieval Europe, people thought that beyond the known world lived tribes of people with wolves' heads or horses' bodies (right), *not so far from some aliens in* Star Trek!

A New World

For the past 32 days, no land had been sighted. Mermaids (probably manatees) had even been seen swimming around the boat, and the crew was close to mutiny. The captain was worried – according to his charts, they should have reached Japan (*left*).

Then, just in time, signs of land appeared – floating branches with fresh leaves, and birds flying overhead. In the early hours of October 12, the lookout spotted a faint shape ahead. Land! It was tiny Watling Island (part of the Bahamas). Just after noon the next day, the Italian captain – Cristóbal Colón (Christopher Columbus) – stepped onto the white coral beach, and thanked God for the safe passage of his crew.

The Wrong Name
In 1507, German mapmaker Martin Waldseemäller (left) coined the name "America" to honor the Italian navigator Amerigo Vespucci (1454–1512). He had read Vespucci's boastful accounts of his explorations. Later, Waldseemäller tried to change the name "America" but it was too late!

A Small World
Christopher Columbus (1451–1506) made four voyages of transatlantic exploration, but died believing his discoveries lay only a short distance from China. Meanwhile, John Cabot (c.1450–1499, *below*), had found a landmass to the north (map on page 24).

By 1513, when Vasco Balboa (c.1475–1519) crossed the Isthmus of Panama and gazed upon the mighty Pacific Ocean, Europeans were coming to realize that Columbus had stumbled across an entirely "New World."

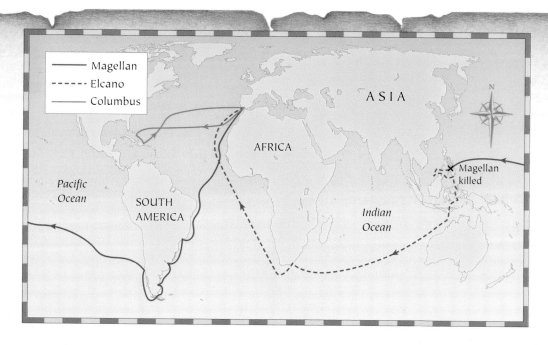

Two of the Greatest (left) *The routes of Columbus' first Atlantic crossing (1492–1493) and Magellan/del Cano's voyage around the globe (1519–1522).*

These two epic voyages changed our understanding of the world forever. One brought America into contact with Europe, the other finally proved that the Earth was round.

Legend:
— Magellan
--- Elcano
— Columbus

Map labels: ASIA · AFRICA · SOUTH AMERICA · Pacific Ocean · Indian Ocean · ✕ Magellan killed

Beach Party (main picture)
When local Caribs met him on the beach, Columbus thought at first they were inhabitants from the fabled island of Cipangu, off the coast of China, just 4,000 miles from Europe!

THE FIRST TIME AROUND

In 1519 Portuguese Ferdinand Magellan (c.1480–1521) left Spain with five ships and 241 men. They found a passage around South America and crossed the Pacific to the Philippines, where Magellan was killed in a local war. One of his officers, Sebastian del Cano, took command. In 1522, with a single vessel and 18 other survivors he made it back to Spain. They had sailed around the world.

MYTH AND REALITY. Columbus was impressed by the Greek myth of Atlantis – a lost Atlantic island which provided the ocean with its name. Columbus found no trace of Atlantis. Instead, he came across the West Indies (*above*), inhabited by friendly Caribs who came out to greet him. Tragically, these gentle people were almost wiped out by European cruelty and disease.

"ALL THAT GLISTENS..."

Columbus's discovery of the New World drew thousands of Spanish adventurers across the Atlantic in search of fame and fortune. In 1526, the ruthless Spanish soldier Francisco Pizarro left Panama to conquer Peru. He failed, but learned of the fabulous gold (*left*) of the crumbling Inca Empire. Returning in 1531 with 263 men and 37 horses, Pizarro struck inland (map on page 18) and seized the Inca leader.

The conquistador (conqueror) collected a huge ransom in gold and silver, then murdered his prisoner. Before long, the entire Inca Empire was in Spanish hands.

THE PRICE OF BEING EXPLORED

The Aztecs of Mexico developed the most vigorous ancient American civilization. Based around the city of Tenochtitlan, it produced wonderful architecture, jewelry, and textiles, and beautiful charts showing its history (*above*). Europeans were less impressed by its religion, which involved human sacrifice.

Beginning in 1518, conquistador Hernán Cortés (1485–1547) overcame the Aztecs in a startling four-year campaign (see map on page 18). Subjected to slavery and decimated by European diseases like smallpox, the Aztec population declined rapidly.

Spaniards plunder Tenochtitlan (left).

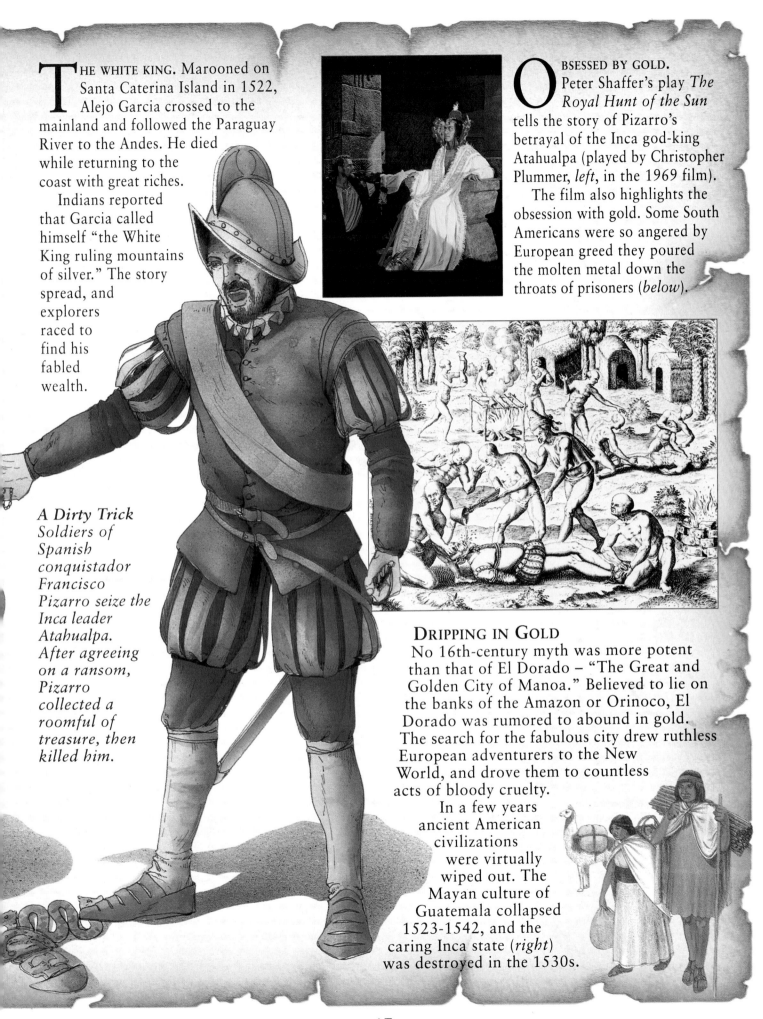

THE WHITE KING. Marooned on Santa Caterina Island in 1522, Alejo Garcia crossed to the mainland and followed the Paraguay River to the Andes. He died while returning to the coast with great riches.

Indians reported that Garcia called himself "the White King ruling mountains of silver." The story spread, and explorers raced to find his fabled wealth.

A Dirty Trick
Soldiers of Spanish conquistador Francisco Pizarro seize the Inca leader Atahualpa. After agreeing on a ransom, Pizarro collected a roomful of treasure, then killed him.

OBSESSED BY GOLD. Peter Shaffer's play *The Royal Hunt of the Sun* tells the story of Pizarro's betrayal of the Inca god-king Atahualpa (played by Christopher Plummer, *left*, in the 1969 film).

The film also highlights the obsession with gold. Some South Americans were so angered by European greed they poured the molten metal down the throats of prisoners (*below*).

DRIPPING IN GOLD

No 16th-century myth was more potent than that of El Dorado – "The Great and Golden City of Manoa." Believed to lie on the banks of the Amazon or Orinoco, El Dorado was rumored to abound in gold. The search for the fabulous city drew ruthless European adventurers to the New World, and drove them to countless acts of bloody cruelty.

In a few years ancient American civilizations were virtually wiped out. The Mayan culture of Guatemala collapsed 1523-1542, and the caring Inca state (*right*) was destroyed in the 1530s.

BEYOND THE SHORE

In 1540, a party of Spanish conquistadors left Quito to explore the land east of the Andes. Upon reaching the Coca River, they built a two-masted ship and sent second-in-command Francisco de Orellana (c. 1490–c. 1546) downstream to find provisions. In February 1542, Orellana sailed into a huge river. Forgetting the others, he rebuilt his boat (*right*) and followed the stream for thousands of miles to the Atlantic (see map, *left*). Without realizing it, he had navigated the world's largest river – the Amazon!

THE CORPS OF DISCOVERY

At the time of the American Revolution (1775–1783), the vast interior of the North American landmass was largely unknown to the government in Washington. To rectify this, in 1804, President Thomas Jefferson got Congress to fund a "Corps of Discovery." Led by Meriwether Lewis (1774–1809) and William Clark (1770–1838) (both *right*), the Corps traveled over 8,000 miles up the Missouri River and over the Rockies to the Pacific Ocean (map on page 19).

UNSUNG HEROES

Explorers were dependent on native guides to help them move quickly across roadless terrain. In North America, as well as providing Europeans with local knowledge of the countryside, the native people taught them to use the snowshoes, toboggans, and canoes that were ideally suited to travel on the continent.

Indiana Jones (far left) *is perhaps Hollywood's most famous discoverer. In his search for the treasures of the past, the daring professor braves the darkest jungles and the hottest deserts.*

MEN WITH A MISSION

In the later 17th century, French Jesuit priests, such as Father René Ménard, explored vast tracts in the region of the Great Lakes, spreading their gospel among the Indian tribes. Meanwhile in 1682, Frenchman Robert de la Salle journeyed down the Mississippi as part of his plan to build a vast French commercial empire stretching from the Great Lakes to the Gulf of Mexico.

Technochtitlan
Santiago
Veracruz
Port of Spain
Panama
Quito
Cajamarca
Macchu Picchu
Cuzco
SOUTH AMERICA

Cortes
Pizarro
Orellana

North America The routes of explorers Lewis and0 Clark, Mackenzie, and La Salle (right).

NORTH AMERICA

St. Louis

New Orleans

Mississippi

— Mackenzie
— Lewis & Clark
— La Salle

SEARCHING FUR TRADE

(*left*) In 1789, fur trader Sir Alexander Mackenzie (1764–1820) set out to find a waterway from Lake Athabaska to the Pacific. He went north to the Slave Lake and followed a river to the sea. Discovering it was the Arctic Ocean, not the Pacific, he named the waterway the River of Disappointment (now the Mackenzie). He finally reached the Pacific on his second trip (1793).

A Trickle Turns to a Flood

The reports of explorers like Lewis and Clark encouraged settlers to head west. Boosted by frenzied railroad building and the Californian gold rush of 1849, thousands more set off in the hope of building a new life (above). But white settlers gained their new land at the expense of the previous owners – the Native Americans.

BEASTS AND BEAUTIES

Since the beginning of time sailors have encountered terrible dangers in the unknown vastness beyond the horizon. None were more terrifying than those faced by Odysseus when returning from the Trojan Wars.

On one side lay Charybdis, the gigantic whirlpool that sucked ships to certain doom. On the other stood the monster Scylla, with six heads and a ring of dogs around her waist. Odysseus steered his ship away from Charybdis, but too close to Scylla. The monster struck and carried off six of his crew. This legend is said to be based on the dangerous Straits of Messina that lie between Sicily and Italy.

The Devil and the Deep Blue Sea
Odysseus passes between Scylla and the fearful Charybdis (above).

AN ARKFUL

European explorers were amazed by the strange creatures they came across on their travels. Marco Polo called crocodiles "serpent monsters" (*left*).

Explorers in Australia thought kangaroos were jumping dogs! Shocked by the number of new species he found in South America, Amerigo Vespucci even found himself doubting the story of Noah's Ark!

SUCKED TO DEATH

Whirlpools occur where two ocean currents meet from opposite directions, or where winds blow against sea currents.

Sailors were right to fear whirlpools, as they could sink a small ship. However, they were always more dangerous in myth than reality.

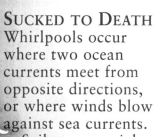

JAWS AND FRIENDS

What fearful monsters lurk in the hidden corners of the Earth? Early explorers really believed that giant squid (*left*) and other terrible creatures might rise from the sea to devour them.

Even today we shudder at a mythical great white shark – "Jaws" – and stare in wonder into the dark depths of Loch Ness (both *right*)!

WATER, WATER EVERYWHERE
Samuel Taylor Coleridge's poem *The Rime of the Ancient Mariner* (1798) tells of the perils that befell a sailor who shot an albatross (*right*), the sailors' lucky bird. It contains the famous lines expressing the great fear of many sailors – dying of thirst:

Water, water, everywhere,
Nor any drop to drink.

Monster Fun! (main picture)
Using a special effects technique called Dynamation, *Ray Harryhausen brought to life a series of fantastic creatures in the Sinbad films.*

DANGEROUS LADIES
Used to only male company, some sailors became frightened of women. As a result, they dreamed up dangerous female monsters. Singing sirens lured seamen onto dangerous rocks. In northern Europe sirens became confused with mermaids (*left*) – half-women, half-fish – that may have been based on seals or dugongs.

In ancient times, Amazons – a tribe of warlike women – were said to dwell beside the Black Sea.

MOBY DICK. Created by the writer Herman Melville (1819–1891) in 1851, the cunning and fierce white whale Moby Dick is perhaps the best-known of all sea monsters. The whale bit off Captain Ahab's leg, and he pursued it around the world until it finally broke his neck and sank his ship. *Moby Dick* was based on the sperm whale (*above*), the largest toothed mammal and known to eat sharks whole!

THE SPICE OF LIFE

Hot Profit
Europeans loved Asian spices, such as pepper, cinnamon, cloves, and nutmeg (above), *which they used in cooking and for medicinal purposes.*

Before Portuguese merchants discovered the sea route around Africa, the profitable spice trade was completely in Arab hands.

Columbus's discoveries suggested that Spain had found the sea route to Asia. In desperation, in 1497 King Manuel I of Portugal ordered Vasco da Gama to follow Dias's course around Africa and proceed to India, a route that had been confirmed by Péro da Covilhão.

Da Gama skirted Africa and, guided by an Arab pilot, crossed to Calicut, India, in May 1498 (see map *below*). Though unimpressed by the Portuguese goods, the Muslim ruler treated the visitors kindly (*right*). Da Gama was delighted to find that for three ducats he could buy pepper worth 80 ducats in Venice. He loaded up 80 tons of pepper and returned home to Portugal to receive a triumphant welcome!

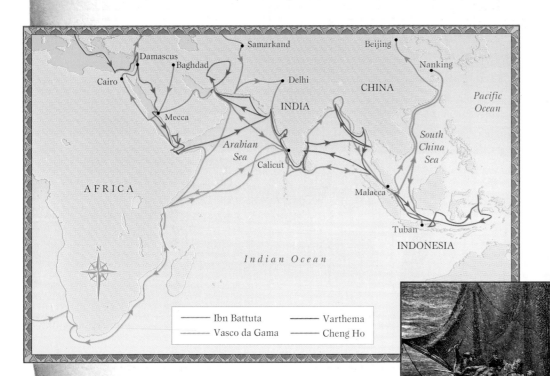

Damascus
Baghdad
Samarkand
Beijing
Nanking
Cairo
Delhi
CHINA
Pacific Ocean
Mecca
INDIA
Arabian Sea
Calicut
South China Sea
AFRICA
Malacca
Tuban
INDONESIA
Indian Ocean

— Ibn Battuta
— Varthema
— Vasco da Gama
— Cheng Ho

BATTUTA THE WANDERER
After its establishment in 622 A.D., Islam spread rapidly throughout the Middle East, North Africa, India, and beyond. Thousands of pilgrims and explorers traveled the Muslim world. The most famous was Ibn Battuta (1304–1368, shown *right* under attack by pirates). Called "the most traveled man on Earth," he journeyed from the Niger River to distant China (*above*).

Long-Distance Pilgrims
Islamic exploration owed much to Mecca, "the house of Allah," as a center for pilgrimage. Pilgrims (right) developed an urge to travel and many wrote descriptions of the places they had visited.

THE FALSE MUSLIM

Following da Gama's epic voyage to India, Europeans quickly penetrated other oriental markets. Many valuable spices, such as nutmeg, came from the Moluccas ("Spice Islands") of Indonesia. The first European to reach there was Italian Lodovico Varthema (d. 1517), who explored Asia, often disguised as a Muslim (see map on page 22).

FROM TRADERS TO CONQUERORS

By the 17th century, Portuguese traders were competing with merchants from Holland, Britain, France, and Spain.

Rival companies established trading posts, such as those at Batavia (Dutch, now Jakarta), Calcutta (British), Goa (Portuguese), and Manila (Spanish). By the 19th century, European powers had used their military might to expand these into colonies. The controversial history of colonial rule has been popularized by such books and films as E.M. Forster's *A Passage to India* (left).

Close to the Wind
An important change in sail design preceded the European voyages of discovery. The square sails of the classical and early medieval period were effective only with a following wind.
The adoption of triangular (or "lateen") sails, first used by Arab vessels in the Mediterranean (right), opened up new routes to navigators.

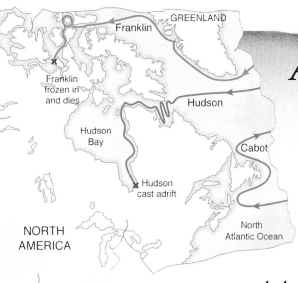

AT THE TOP OF THE WORLD

Explorers dreamed of finding a route to Asia around the north of America, like Magellan's around the south. In 1610, a group of English merchants hired explorer Henry Hudson (c.1550–1611) to find this elusive Northwest Passage.

On entering what is now Hudson's Bay (see map, *left*), Hudson believed that he had reached the Pacific Ocean. When further exploration revealed no open sea, his exhausted crew mutinied. In the spring of 1611, Hudson, his son, and seven sailors were cast adrift in a small open boat (*main picture*). They all perished in the icy conditions.

The Great Dane
In 1728 Danish explorer Vitus Bering (c.1680–1741, left) discovered the strait dividing Asia from North America which now bears his name. Bering was in the service of the Russian Navy. The Russian Tsar, Peter the Great, had ordered Bering to chart the region as part of his plan to extend Russia's power into northeastern Siberia.

DRIFTING TO FAME
Fridtjof Nansen (1861–1930, *right*) made the first crossing of Greenland (1888). From 1893–1896 the bold Norwegian demonstrated the currents in the Northeast Passage by sailing his ship *Fram* from Norway to the Laptev Sea, and letting her drift back again in the pack ice (see map on page 40).

These exploits made Nansen the leading Polar explorer of his day. Other explorers, including Scott and Amundsen, eagerly sought his advice.

WHITE DEATH
The weather was not the only hazard encountered by explorers in the Arctic Circle. There were also huge and ferocious polar bears (*left*). Eight feet (2.5 m) long and weighing up to 1,543 pounds (700 kgs), they can kill a man with a single swipe from their massive clawed paws.

Cast Adrift (main picture)
Captain Henry Hudson is abandoned in a small, open boat with his son and seven loyal members of his crew. They were never seen again. It was another 250 years before anyone successfully negotiated the Northwest Passage.

FRANKLY USELESS. In 1845, Sir John Franklin led an expedition to trace the Northwest Passage (map on page 24). But his crew soon fell prey to the Arctic winter when their ship was frozen in. Many died from lead poisoning from canned food, others from scurvy. Over the next few months, all 134 men perished.

When his body was finally found, Franklin was dubbed a national hero by the press in Britain, even though he had failed miserably!

Bitten by Cold
Early polar explorers suffered terrible hardships. Only a few, such as Nansen, wisely copied local Inuit techniques. The worst peril was frostbite (above), the freezing of body tissues. It commonly led to explorers' toes and fingers dropping off. When the flesh thawed, there was the further danger of gangrene.

Franklin's rescue party *found a sad trail of skeletons – and Franklin's dying words (left).*

GONE MISSING
In 1850, Robert McClure (1807–1873) entered the Arctic through the Bering Strait to look for the missing explorer Sir John Franklin.

McClure abandoned his ship in the ice and was eventually rescued three years later. Led back through Baffin Bay, he became the first explorer to complete the Northwest Passage.

LAPTEV'S LEAP
When the Russian explorer Khariton Laptev (1680–1732) tried to sail around the bleak Taymyr Peninsula, his boat became trapped in the ice. Undaunted, Laptev and his intrepid crew abandoned their ship and in two days covered the 15 miles to dry land by leaping across the icebergs (*right*)!

Woolly Warmers
Before the days of specially manufactured clothing, explorers relied on wool and leather to protect them from the freezing weather. Leather cracked in the cold and wool froze solid when wet.

THE GREAT INTERIOR

Europeans were fascinated by the remote Tibetan city of Lhasa. Cut off from the outside world by snow-covered mountains, it is dominated by the mystical Potala Palace, a huge castlelike building with roofs of gold. China closed Tibet to foreigners in 1792, but several daring adventurers broke the ban. The most remarkable was the Englishwoman Alexandra David-Neale.

Darkening her face with cocoa and dying her hair, Neale dressed as an Indian nun and set out for Lhasa on a yak.

In 1922, the fearless 54-year-old Buddhist scholar became the first European woman to enter the sacred city (*main picture*).

One Hump or Two?
We usually imagine camels in the deserts of Arabia, but the two-humped variety (above) was just as essential to travelers in Central Asia who needed to cross the vast Gobi desert.

SUPER SURVEYOR
Nain Singh, a 19th-century surveyor, was probably the most energetic mapmaker of all time. In 1866, he traveled 1,200 miles through Tibet in disguise, mapping the route to the forbidden city of Lhasa (see map on page 27). The next year he left on a seven-year trip that resulted in the first-ever scientific survey of Tibet and the upper reaches of the Indus River.

On the Hoof
Between 1867 and 1877 Nikolai Przewalski (1839–1888) made five scientific expeditions into Central Asia (above). His greatest discovery was the last remaining species of wild horse (left), named Equus Przevalskii *in his honor.*

JOURNEYS IN THE MIND. No imaginary journey is more famous than that of Lemuel Gulliver, the hero of Jonathan Swift's *Gulliver's Travels* (1726). The book was written as a criticism of human nature but became a children's classic. Gulliver visits Lilliput (inhabited by tiny people, *right*), Brobdingnag (a land of giants), the flying island of Laputa, the Island of Sorcerers, and a country shared between reasonable horses and brutal human-looking Yahoos.

FURTHEST CORNERS

Before the travels of 19th-century explorers Nikolai Przewalski and Ney Elias, the vast barren reaches of Mongolia were largely unknown to the outside world. Outer Mongolia (*page 26*) and the city of Timbuktu, on the edge of the Sahara (*left*), are still bywords for places that are impossibly far away.

Chaps with Maps
Several travelers and cartographers helped open up Central Asia to the world. Among the most important were Father Bento de Gões (1562–1607), who followed the route of Marco Polo, Francis Younghusband (1863–1942), who trekked across the Gobi desert, Przewalski (Przhevalsky), and Nain Singh (see right for map).

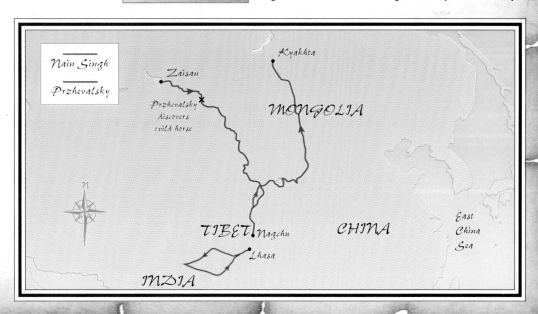

ISLANDS AND ISLANDERS

In 1778, when he left to find western access to the Northwest Passage, Captain James Cook was already the most famous explorer of his generation. In two monumental voyages (1768–1771 and 1772–1775, see map *below*) he had charted vast areas of the south Pacific, including Tahiti, Tonga, New Zealand, and eastern Australia, in his search for a great undiscovered southern continent.

On his third voyage, Cook entered the Bering Strait before being forced back by ice. He called twice at Hawaii. On the second visit he went to examine the theft of a rowboat, and was stabbed to death.

Able Tasman
While looking for "New Holland" (Australia), the Dutch explorer Abel Tasman (1603–1659, above fighting off a native attack) was the first European to see Tasmania and New Zealand. He also explored extensively in the Indian and Pacific Oceans.

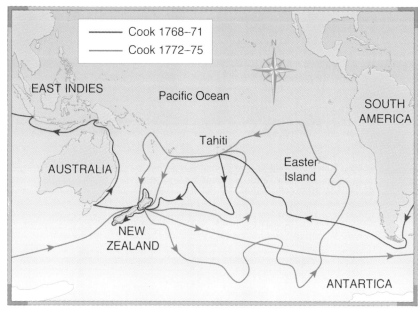

Map legend:
— Cook 1768–71
— Cook 1772–75

EAST INDIES · Pacific Ocean · SOUTH AMERICA · Tahiti · Easter Island · AUSTRALIA · NEW ZEALAND · ANTARTICA

ISLAND HOPPERS

The Maori people of New Zealand (*below*) originally came from islands farther out in the Pacific. Their cultural heritage, rich in song, dance, and storytelling, was severely disrupted by European settlers.

Long before the arrival of Europeans, they and other inhabitants of the Pacific had used stars, currents, and wave patterns to navigate the great ocean. Cook himself used a map drawn by an *arii* (priest) from the Society Islands.

Men on the Moon?
Captain Cook beside the gigantic Neolithic carvings on Easter Island, Polynesia.
When Europeans discovered the island on Easter Sunday, 1722, they found that the inhabitants believed their nearest neighbors lived on the moon.

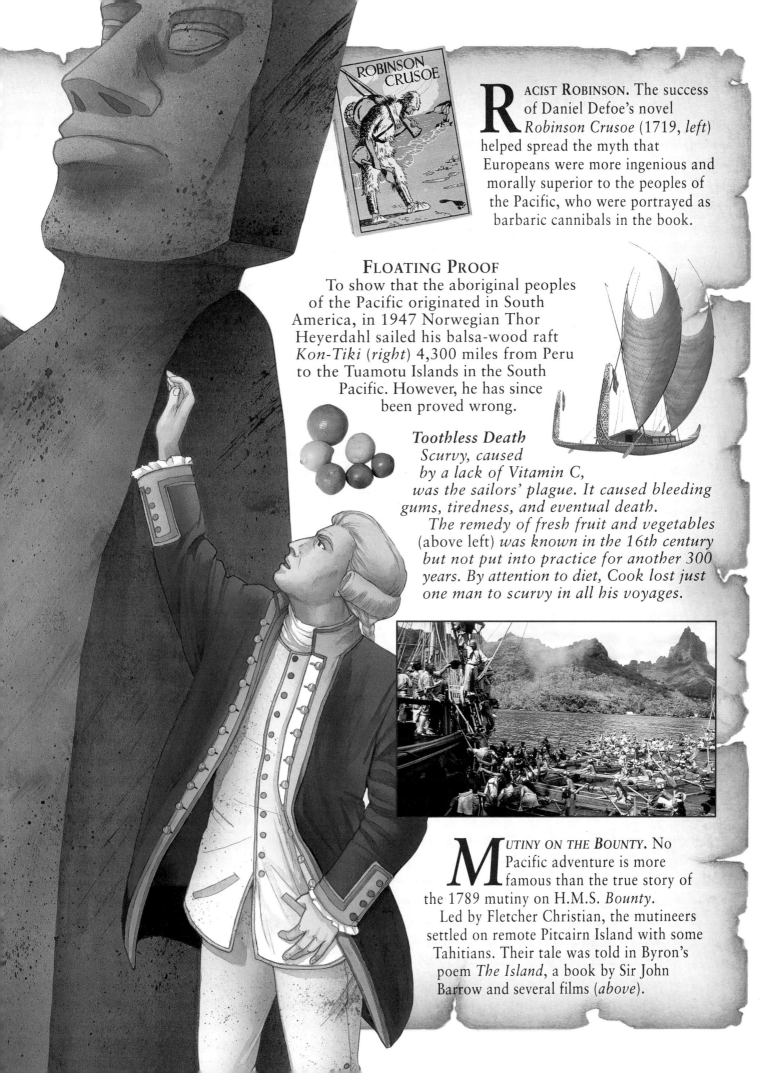

RACIST ROBINSON. The success of Daniel Defoe's novel *Robinson Crusoe* (1719, *left*) helped spread the myth that Europeans were more ingenious and morally superior to the peoples of the Pacific, who were portrayed as barbaric cannibals in the book.

FLOATING PROOF
To show that the aboriginal peoples of the Pacific originated in South America, in 1947 Norwegian Thor Heyerdahl sailed his balsa-wood raft *Kon-Tiki* (*right*) 4,300 miles from Peru to the Tuamotu Islands in the South Pacific. However, he has since been proved wrong.

Toothless Death
Scurvy, caused by a lack of Vitamin C, was the sailors' plague. It caused bleeding gums, tiredness, and eventual death.
The remedy of fresh fruit and vegetables (above left) was known in the 16th century but not put into practice for another 300 years. By attention to diet, Cook lost just one man to scurvy in all his voyages.

MUTINY ON THE BOUNTY. No Pacific adventure is more famous than the true story of the 1789 mutiny on H.M.S. *Bounty.* Led by Fletcher Christian, the mutineers settled on remote Pitcairn Island with some Tahitians. Their tale was told in Byron's poem *The Island*, a book by Sir John Barrow and several films (*above*).

ACROSS THE EMPTY LAND

When the search party arrived at Cooper Creek, they were surprised to find the local Aborigines greatly excited. They had something to show the visitors.

Following the Aborigines to their camp, the party found John King – or what was left of him. He was burned black by the sun, as thin as a skeleton, and hardly able to speak. But he was at least alive – the only survivor of the ill-fated Burke-Willis expedition that had made the first crossing of Australia by white settlers (see map on page 31, *opposite*).

SUCCESS AND FAILURE (see maps on page 31) Explorers Edward John Eyre (1815–1901) and Friedrich William Ludwig Leichardt (1813–1848, left) met with very different fates. Eyre traveled widely with an Aboriginal companion and became the first Protector of Aborigines. Leichardt, a German explorer, disappeared while trying to make the first east-west crossing of Australia. Charles Sturt (1795–1869), determined to find a giant inland sea, led an expedition into central Australia. Defeated by the heat of the Simpson desert and scurvy, his party was forced to return to Adelaide.

Conquering the Outback
It wasn't just the dry heat that made central Australia such a tough place to explore. The Aborigines, understandably angered at the white men stealing their land, sometimes launched vicious attacks. The bush (top) was undermined by rat-holes, in which horses and camels frequently broke their legs. Deadly snakes, spiders (below), scorpions, and biting centipedes lurked on the ground. In the north, crocodiles swam in the swamps while mosquitoes hovered overhead.

ARRIVAL AND ADAPTATION Australia's first inhabitants crossed to continent many thousands of years B.C. As the polar ice cap were much larger than today sea levels much lower, they we able to make most of the jour on foot. As the climate gradua changed, they adapted to the increasingly dry conditions.

The Aboriginal knowledge bushcraft and waterholes pro indispensab to Europe explorers. Those wh ignored it like Burke a Wills – paid their lives.

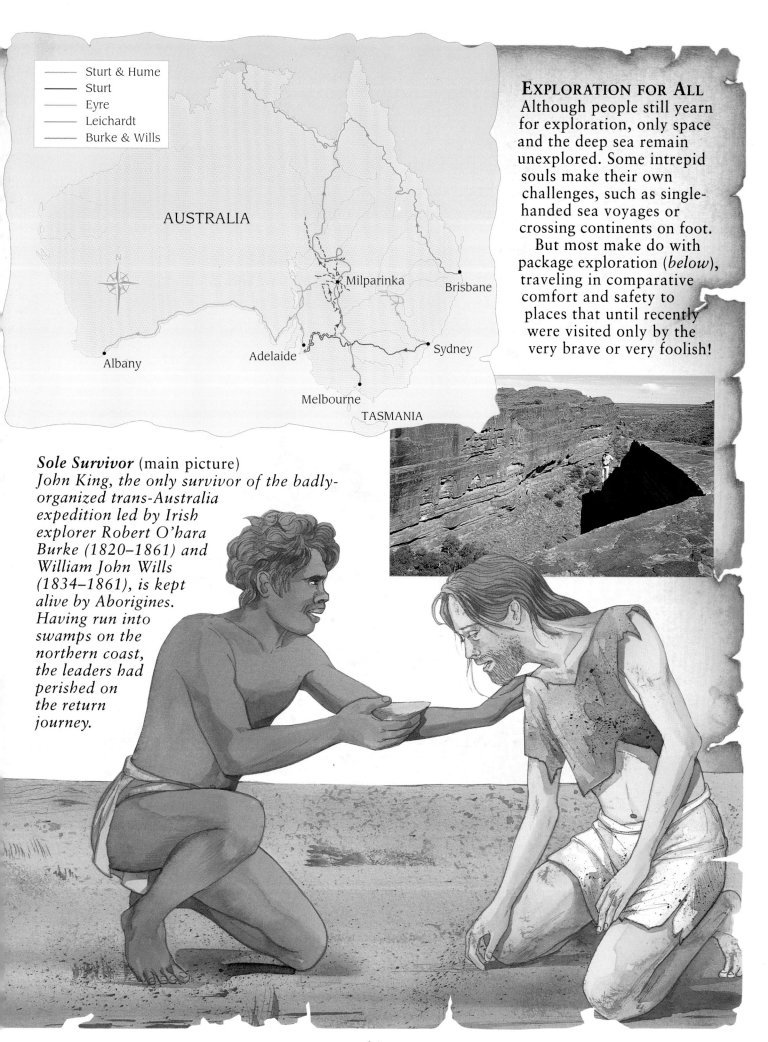

Map legend:
- Sturt & Hume
- Sturt
- Eyre
- Leichardt
- Burke & Wills

AUSTRALIA

Albany
Adelaide
Milparinka
Brisbane
Sydney
Melbourne
TASMANIA

EXPLORATION FOR ALL
Although people still yearn for exploration, only space and the deep sea remain unexplored. Some intrepid souls make their own challenges, such as single-handed sea voyages or crossing continents on foot.

But most make do with package exploration (*below*), traveling in comparative comfort and safety to places that until recently were visited only by the very brave or very foolish!

Sole Survivor (main picture)
John King, the only survivor of the badly-organized trans-Australia expedition led by Irish explorer Robert O'hara Burke (1820–1861) and William John Wills (1834–1861), is kept alive by Aborigines. Having run into swamps on the northern coast, the leaders had perished on the return journey.

WHERE ON EARTH ARE WE?

Knowing exactly where you are is a matter of life or death to an explorer. The amazing adventures of English aviator Amy Johnson (1903–1941) were a triumph of solo navigation, and carried the daredevil spirit of exploration into the 20th century. In 1930, with only 100 hours' flying experience, Johnson bought a secondhand Gypsy Moth for $900 (*main picture*) and set out to become the first woman to fly solo from England to Australia. She completed the incredible journey in 19 days. On the way she flew blind through sandstorms, repaired her plane with plaster, and used judo to fight off amorous Arabs!

Drake's Compass
Sir Francis Drake used this all-in-one compass, tide tables, and solar and star tables (above).

THE LAST LOCKUP. In sailor's slang, Davy Jones was the evil spirit of the deep, sometimes associated with the Devil himself. "Davy Jones' Locker" is the bottom of the ocean, the final resting place of sunken ships and sailors who have drowned or been buried at sea.

Once a ship got caught in a storm (*left*), there was little a captain could do except batten down the hatches and pray for fair weather.

Sextant (left)
The sextant, which came into use in the mid-18th century, is one of the most accurate instruments for finding a vessel's latitude.

Mechanical Aids
In ancient times, sailors navigated by observing the night sky and by studying tides and winds.
Later, instruments such as the quadrant (left) and the astrolabe (right), were used for fixing a ship's latitude (distance above or below the equator), by measuring the angle of the sun or stars above the horizon.

Quadrant

Astrolabe

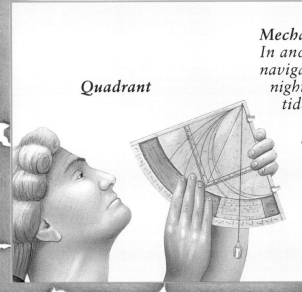

VANISHING BRITS
More than any other nation, England specializes in heroic failure. John Cabot was swallowed up by the Atlantic Ocean (1498), and Mungo Park by the Niger River (1806, *see page 34*).

Henry Hudson vanished in the bay that bears his name (1611). Cold undid Sir Henry Franklin (1847), and Robert Scott in the Antarctic (1912, *right*).

HIMALAYAN PARADISE
Not often does a film add a new world to the language. But this was the case with *The Lost Horizon* (1936, remade in 1972, *below*), written by James Hilton.

Shangri-La, the movie's heavenly valley in the Himalayas, nowadays means any earthly paradise.

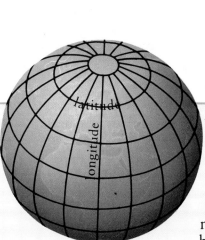

Navigators plot their position using lines of longitude (east-west) and latitude (north-south).

CLOCKING THE MILES
Longitude is an east-west position on the surface of the Earth. As the Earth spins once every 24 hours, distance can be measured in time difference. One hour is 15° longitude.

However, longitude could not be accurately measured until the invention of the chronometer (a very accurate clock) in the mid-18th century. A 19th-century chronometer is shown on the *right*.

ALONG THE GREAT RIVERS

In 1805, the British Government asked Doctor Mungo Park to return to Africa to trace the course of the mighty Niger River. He gave up his practice and left for Gambia.

By the time Park set out down the river in his home-made boat, 36 of his party of 40 had been hit with malaria and dysentery. Five months later he was ambushed – the local Bussa people thought his party meant to attack them, and not understanding the white flag shown by Park, they showered his boat with poisoned arrows – leaving just one survivor.

Today's adventurers enjoy the thrill of shooting the rapids on a stretch of the Zambezi River (top).

But these fast-flowing waters could smash an explorer's raft to pieces in minutes.

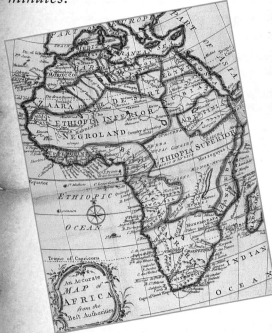

A Complete Blank
Gibson's 1793 Map of Africa (above) reveals how little was known of the African interior by the outside world at this time.

TRACING THE MIGHTY NIGER
Mungo Park (1771–1806), the Scottish explorer, made his name with the publication of his *Travels in the Interior of Africa* (1799). The book described his journeys to discover the source of the Niger River (map on page 37). But despite Park's findings, scholars still believed the Niger joined up with the Nile River, thousands of miles east!

THE CITY OF GOLD. Legend said Timbuktu's streets were paved with gold. Arab traders, crossing the Sahara by camel (*left*) in the 15th century, fueled the legend with tales of fabulous riches at the court of King Mansa Musa. But when Scottish explorer Alexander Laing (1793–1826) got there in the 19th century, he found only mud huts.

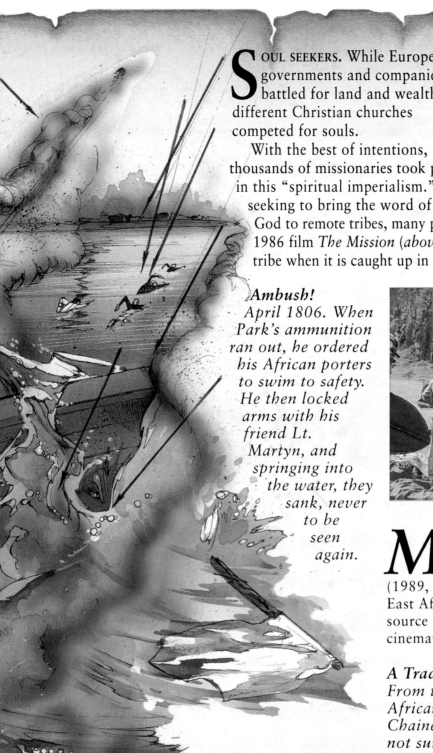

S OUL SEEKERS. While European governments and companies battled for land and wealth, different Christian churches competed for souls.

With the best of intentions, thousands of missionaries took part in this "spiritual imperialism." In seeking to bring the word of God to remote tribes, many performed acts of daring exploration. In the 1986 film *The Mission (above)*, two priests side with a South American tribe when it is caught up in a war between imperial powers.

Ambush!
April 1806. When Park's ammunition ran out, he ordered his African porters to swim to safety. He then locked arms with his friend Lt. Martyn, and springing into the water, they sank, never to be seen again.

M OUNTAINS OF THE MOON. The rivalry of Sir Richard Burton and John Speke inspired the film *Mountains of the Moon* (1989, *above*). Set against the lonely beauty of East Africa, where the explorers searched for the source of the Nile, it is an unusually accurate cinematic tribute to the heroic age of exploration.

A Trade in Human Misery (below)
From the 1500s to the 1800s, 12 million Africans were shipped across the Atlantic. Chained together in terrible conditions, it is not surprising that 2 million died on the way.

BOUNTY HUNTERS
Though many explorers were drawn to Africa out of curiosity, others went in search of wealth, in the form of gold, spices – and slaves. Though Arab slavers had operated in Africa since medieval times, the slave trade became big business to Europe in the 17th century, providing labor for the sugar and cotton plantations of the New World.

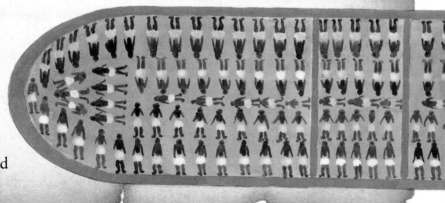

"DR. LIVINGSTONE, I PRESUME"

David Livingstone, the greatest of all African explorers, was missing. He had left England in 1865 to confirm Speke's belief that Lake Victoria was the source of the Nile (map on page 37). By 1871, no definite news had been received from him for three years.

The New York Herald sent its experienced reporter Henry Stanley to Africa in search of the great man. When the two met at Ujiji on Lake Tanganyika, Stanley uttered his famous greeting, "Doctor Livingstone, I presume?"

Angelic Falls (above)
From 1853–1856 David Livingstone traveled 5,500 miles in his journey across the African continent. In November 1855, he came across the Victoria Falls – "scenes so lovely must have been gazed upon by angels."

THE GREAT DELIVERER. From the time of the Crusades, European explorers were fascinated by the myth of the great Christian priest-king Prester John (*right*). Originally believed to be in Asia, by the 1330s his kingdom had moved to Ethiopia.

SNEAKY SPEKE

The waters of the Nile River had cradled early civilization, but their origins were not discovered until the 19th century. The "Nile Quest" was solved by John Speke (1827–1864, *left*), who in 1858 went off on his own to Lake Victoria while exploring East Africa with Sir Richard Burton (1821–1890) (see map on page 37). The discovery led to a bitter quarrel between the two men which ended only with Speke's accidental shooting in 1864.

Dressing For the Part
To protect them against the rigors of Africa, Europeans wore special clothing such as pith helmets, safari jackets, and snake- and leech-proof boots.

Missing, Presumed Dead
Henry Stanley (1841–1904) finds Dr. David Livingstone (1813–1873) alive at Ujiji on Lake Tanganyika. Stanley went on to explore large areas of eastern Africa, especially around Lakes Victoria and Tanganyika (see map).

	Park
	Burton & Speke
	Rohlfs
	Stanley
	Stanley
	Stanley
	Foureau

Algiers · Tripoli
Timbuktu
AFRICA
Nile
Niger
Lagos
Congo
Atlantic Ocean
Lake Victoria
Lake Tanjanyika

FORGOTTEN HEROES
African guides, bearers, and negotiators played a vital role in the exploration of the continent. A big expedition relied on over 300 paid African workers (*right*), organized by a team leader, or *kirangazi*. The greatest *kirangazi*, nicknamed "Bombay," deserves as much credit as Speke for discovering the source of the Nile.

JUNGLE PETTICOATS
In a long, tight-waisted dress and carrying an umbrella, Mary Kingsley (1862–1900) was a remarkable sight traveling around West Africa in search of scientific information. Once, after wading through a swamp, she emerged with a string of blood-sucking leeches around her neck (*above*). She supported herself by trading and wrote about her experiences in two best-selling books.

THE WHITE MAN'S GRAVE
European diseases wrought terrible havoc on the peoples of the New World. In Africa it was the Europeans who suffered: Thousands died of malaria, sleeping sickness, and other African diseases. Sleeping sickness, spread by the tsetse fly (*right*), also infected horses and oxen, so they couldn't be used to carry supplies and equipment.

THE SCRAMBLE FOR AFRICA

A flotilla of small boats, including a dismantled 80-foot steamboat (*left*), were being carried hundreds of miles across the high plains between the Congo and the White Nile. The sight was one of the most extraordinary Africa had ever seen.

The purpose of Jean-Baptiste Marchand's bizarre expedition was to claim the upper Nile for France and prevent British expansion from Egypt. Marchand duly hoisted the French flag at Fashoda in 1898 and waited to see what would happen. A few months later, General Kitchener arrived with a large British force. Only skillful diplomacy prevented war and the two European powers divided large tracts of northeast Africa between them.

Within 20 years, small groups of explorers had led two full-scale military expeditions to back up territorial claims.

KING SOLOMON'S MINES. In 1885, novelist Sir Henry Rider Haggard wrote the ultimate novel about African exploration. *King Solomon's Mines*, set in southern Africa, tells how a trio of Englishmen overcome numerous perils to restore an African king to his rightful inheritance. Finally, they discover the long-lost treasure of King Solomon and return home as wealthy men. The book was made into a film, starring Richard Chamberlain (*above*), in 1985.

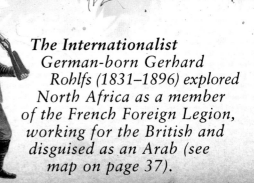

The Internationalist
German-born Gerhard Rohlfs (1831–1896) explored North Africa as a member of the French Foreign Legion, working for the British and disguised as an Arab (see map on page 37).

THE BRITISH AND THE BOERS

Dutch farmers (known as "Boers") were the first Europeans to settle in Africa. Shortly after the British bought South Africa in 1814, the Boers left on a "Great Trek" north to establish their own republics. However, envious of the Boers' gold fields, the British were drawn into the long and costly Boer War (1899–1901, *far right*).

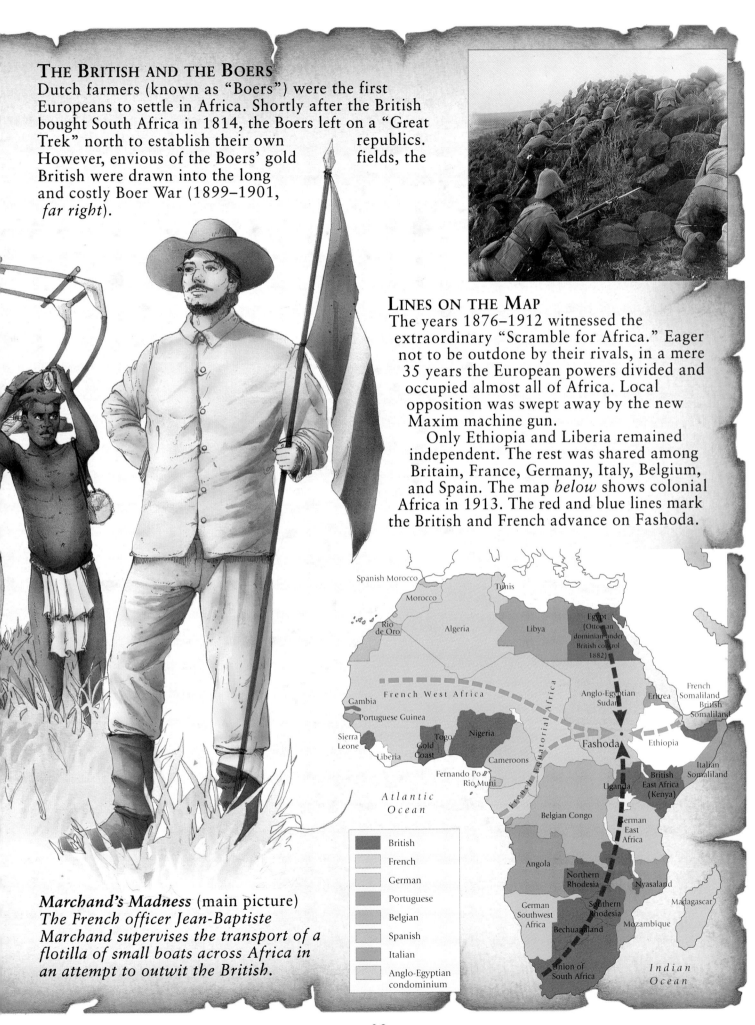

LINES ON THE MAP

The years 1876–1912 witnessed the extraordinary "Scramble for Africa." Eager not to be outdone by their rivals, in a mere 35 years the European powers divided and occupied almost all of Africa. Local opposition was swept away by the new Maxim machine gun.

Only Ethiopia and Liberia remained independent. The rest was shared among Britain, France, Germany, Italy, Belgium, and Spain. The map *below* shows colonial Africa in 1913. The red and blue lines mark the British and French advance on Fashoda.

Spanish Morocco
Morocco
Tunis
Rio de Oro
Algeria
Libya
Egypt (Ottoman dominion under British control 1882)
French West Africa
Gambia
Portuguese Guinea
Sierra Leone
Liberia
Togo
Gold Coast
Nigeria
Cameroons
Fernando Po
Rio Muni
Anglo-Egyptian Sudan
French Equatorial Africa
Fashoda
Eritrea
French Somaliland
British Somaliland
Ethiopia
Italian Somaliland
Uganda
British East Africa (Kenya)
Belgian Congo
German East Africa
Atlantic Ocean
Angola
Northern Rhodesia
Nyasaland
German Southwest Africa
Southern Rhodesia
Bechuanaland
Mozambique
Madagascar
Union of South Africa
Indian Ocean

Legend:
- British
- French
- German
- Portuguese
- Belgian
- Spanish
- Italian
- Anglo-Egyptian condominium

***Marchand's Madness** (main picture)*
The French officer Jean-Baptiste Marchand supervises the transport of a flotilla of small boats across Africa in an attempt to outwit the British.

NORTH AND SOUTH

Norwegian Roald Amundsen left the Bay of Whales and took a new route up the Axel Heiberg Glacier. Robert Scott's English party set out from McMurdo Sound, following the path pioneered by Shackleton two years previously. The race to the South Pole was on.

Amundsen traveled on skis and dog sleds. He reached the Pole a month before Scott and swiftly returned to base. Meanwhile, Scott and his five colleagues reached their destination on foot and turned for the long trudge home. The weather worsened. Dispirited and exhausted, they made painfully slow progress. Two men died.

Finally, 150 miles from base, the four remaining Englishmen froze to death in their tent while the blizzard raged outside.

"Mine at Last"
American Robert Peary (1856–1920, left) said he was the first explorer to lead a party to the North Pole, arriving on April 6, 1909. There are still those who dispute his claim.

A HEROIC MESSAGE

The fame of Robert Scott (1868–1912) rests as much on what he wrote in his diary as what he achieved. A search party found the diary beside his frozen body. Its famous final entry – "For God's sake look after our people" – touched the hearts of the British public and made Scott an instant hero.

GREAT **S**COTT! Supported by composer Ralph Vaughan Williams's moving music, *Scott of the Antarctic* (1949, *left*), reinforced the myth of Scott as a doomed hero rather than a stubborn amateur.

THE ODDBALL EXPLORER

In ordinary life Sir Ernest Henry Shackleton (1874–1922) was an oddball. Fortunately for him, he did not lead an ordinary life.

He made his name as a brave and inspiring leader of Antarctic expeditions. None achieved their goal. On one he turned back 97 miles from the Pole.

On another, his ship the *Endurance* was crushed by ice (*left*) and he had to sail an open boat 800 miles across the icy Southern Ocean to safety.

Antarctic routes (above), *including that of Vivian Fuchs, who reached the South Pole using motor sleds.*

The Pole! (main picture) *December 14, 1911. Roald Amundsen (1872–1928) arrives at the South Pole after a two-month crossing of the frozen continent by dog sled and skis. He beat Scott by 35 days.*

WISDOM OF THE INUITS

The traditions and practices of the Inuit people of the frozen north, originally known as Eskimos ("raw meat eaters"), were adopted by all wise Polar explorers. Peary relied heavily on Inuit assistance in his Arctic expeditions.

Amundsen's victory over Scott in the race to the South Pole owed much to his use of traditional dog sleds (*right*).

FROZEN FANTASY. As late as 1973, Walt Disney still saw the Arctic as a credible setting for a land stuck in a time warp. *The Island at the Top of the World* tells the story of explorers who travel to the Arctic by balloon and find a fantasy valley inhabited by Vikings. Pursued by killer whales, the party eventually escapes on an iceberg! Until Peary's journey in 1909, there was fierce argument about what was at the North Pole. Because the sun never sets at the Pole in summer, some scientists believed it was a warm paradise like the biblical garden of Eden!

In Edgar Rice Burrough's story, *The Land That Time Forgot* (filmed in 1974, *right*), a polar island is inhabited by prehistoric monsters.

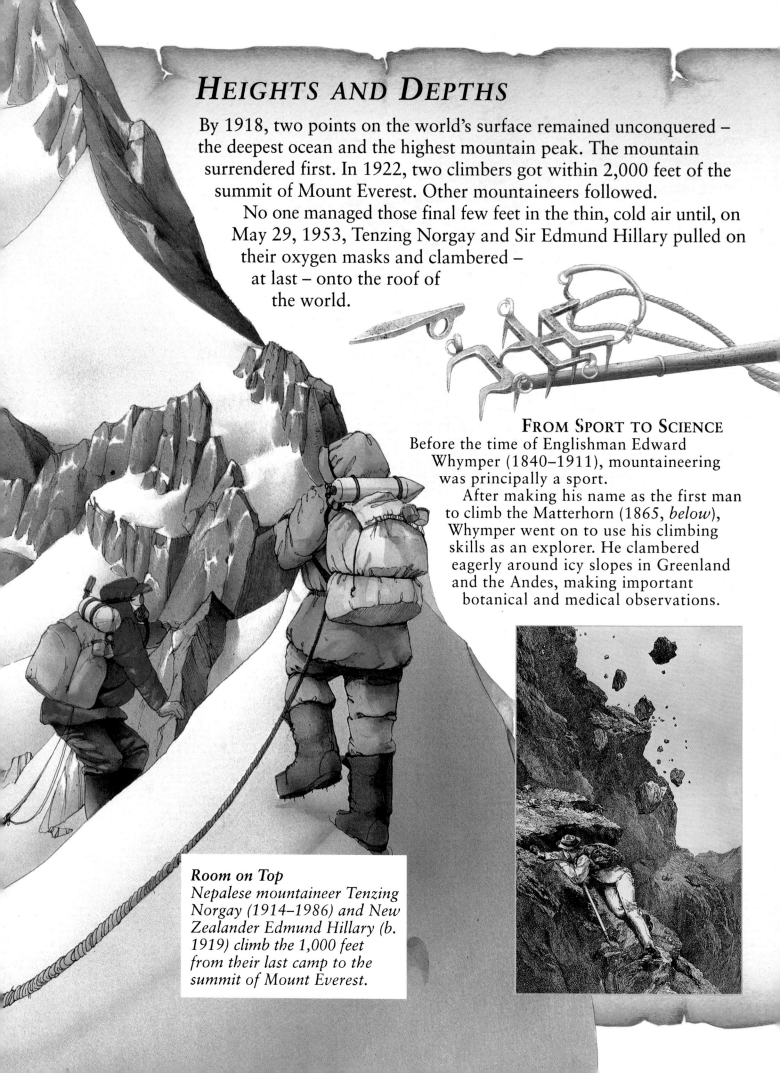

HEIGHTS AND DEPTHS

By 1918, two points on the world's surface remained unconquered – the deepest ocean and the highest mountain peak. The mountain surrendered first. In 1922, two climbers got within 2,000 feet of the summit of Mount Everest. Other mountaineers followed.

No one managed those final few feet in the thin, cold air until, on May 29, 1953, Tenzing Norgay and Sir Edmund Hillary pulled on their oxygen masks and clambered – at last – onto the roof of the world.

FROM SPORT TO SCIENCE

Before the time of Englishman Edward Whymper (1840–1911), mountaineering was principally a sport.

After making his name as the first man to climb the Matterhorn (1865, *below*), Whymper went on to use his climbing skills as an explorer. He clambered eagerly around icy slopes in Greenland and the Andes, making important botanical and medical observations.

Room on Top
Nepalese mountaineer Tenzing Norgay (1914–1986) and New Zealander Edmund Hillary (b. 1919) climb the 1,000 feet from their last camp to the summit of Mount Everest.

INTO THE ABYSS

When mountaineer Edward Whymper camped on the slopes of Cotopaxi Volcano in Ecuador, he found the rubber groundsheet on the floor of his tent was melting! That night, he scrambled to the very rim of the volcano and peered down at the glowing, molten mass below.

However, no one has yet journeyed into the 2200° F heat of a live volcano (*top*).

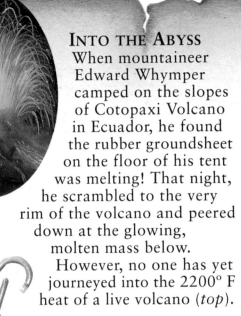

Get a Grip
Two vital pieces of moutaineering equipment are ice picks and crampons (worn on the boot) (left).

VERNE'S JOURNEYS. Frenchman Jules Verne (1828–1905) produced an incomparable series of fantasy exploration novels. They include *Journey to the Center of the Earth* (1864), *Around the World in Eighty Days* (1873), and *Twenty-Thousand Leagues Under the Sea* (1870).

Terrors of the Deep?
The film of 20,000 Leagues Under the Sea (above) began a mini-cult of deep-sea adventure films, of which The Abyss *(1989, right) is one of the most recent.*

Dive, Dive, Dive!
The Turtle (right), built by American David Bushnell, was one of the first submarines.

GOING DOWN

The bathysphere *Trieste* (*below*), in which Jacques Piccard and Don Walsh sank to the deepest point in the ocean, the Marianas Trench, in 1960. The men sat in the tiny capsule at the bottom.

Viewing dome —

DEEP MAPPING

Investigation of marine life and geological structure on the ocean floor began in the 18th century. Three 20th-century developments gave it added importance: (1) the discovery of undersea oil fields; (2) the realization that the Earth's surface comprises gigantic moving plates; (3) the need to monitor ecological changes.

As a result, a variety of submarines, submersibles (such as *Deep Flight One*, *right*), and satellites have now mapped the underwater world almost as accurately as the surface.

"To Boldly Go..."

Space is the final frontier, the explorer's ultimate and infinite goal.
Even before exploration of our own planet was complete, people started to investigate other worlds. *Sputnik I*, the first man-made satellite, orbited the Earth in 1957. Three years later the Soviets launched Yuri Gagarin into orbit. In 1966 *Venera 3* crash-landed on Venus. When astronauts Neil Armstrong and Buzz Aldrin (*left*) became the first humans to walk on the moon in 1969, they achieved a thousand-year-old human dream.

Space stations and unmanned voyages of discovery to distant planets followed. At great expense, we are gradually beginning to piece together a picture of our larger environment. The last and greatest age of exploration has begun.

MOON DREAMS. In 165 A.D. Lucian of Samos said moon travelers would find a huge mirror suspended over a well! H.G. Wells's novel *The First Men in the Moon* (1901) described explorers finding small humanoid moon-creatures (*right*).

Fifty-eight years later the Soviet probe *Luna 2* hit the moon. Finally, ten years later, American astronauts confirmed that there were no moon-men or mirrors – only dust and rocks!

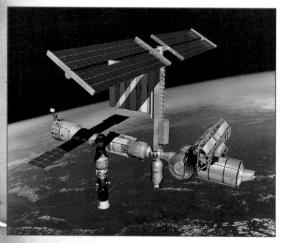

Living in Space
Space Station Alpha (*above*) will be the first continuously occupied space station, a vital stepping stone toward future crewed missions.

Burning Money
The enormous cost of putting rockets like *Saturn V* (*above*) into space led to the space shuttle. But at $250 million per flight, they are just as expensive.

Comet Chaser
Giotto (right) *was one of many probes that studied Halley's Comet in 1986.*

Robot Explorers

For centuries, humans had dreamed up strange creatures from Mars, but when the Viking probes (below) touched down on the surface of the red planet in 1976, no signs of life were found. However, such probes have proved that exploration is possible without the huge risk and expense of putting humans into space.

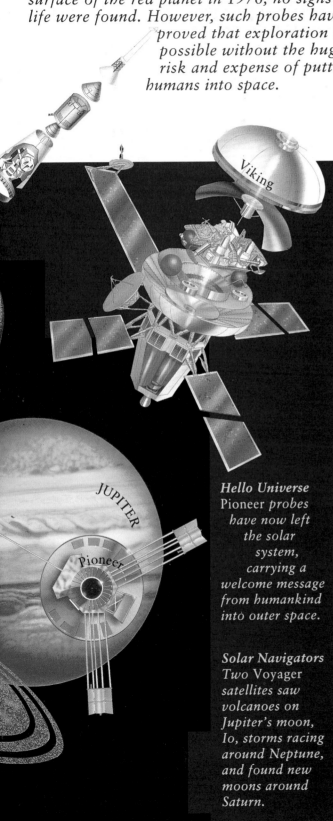

Viking

JUPITER

Pioneer

*Hello Universe
Pioneer probes have now left the solar system, carrying a welcome message from humankind into outer space.*

*Solar Navigators
Two Voyager satellites saw volcanoes on Jupiter's moon, Io, storms racing around Neptune, and found new moons around Saturn.*

SMALL, GREEN, AND SLIMY?

Past generations inhabited unknown regions with mermaids, sea monsters, and giants.

They also wondered what strange creatures inhabited the heavens, like this creature from Sirius (the Dog Star), drawn in the 18th century (*right*).

Today, we fill the distant universe with creatures of our own imagination.

*Friend or Foe?
If we do meet other intelligent lifeforms, will they be friendly, like E.T. (left)? And will we conquer or wipe them out like so many species and peoples on our own planet?*

BEAM ME UP SCOTTY. As a T.V. series and films, *Star Trek* (*below*) remains the most popular modern exploration fantasy. Are the heroics of explorers on the edge of the universe so different from those of their 15th-century counterparts on the edge of the Atlantic?

We have come a long way from our prehistoric ancestors trekking across the Earth, but we still wonder – what is out there – and can we beat it?

EXPLORERS' GLOSSARY

Aborigines The original people of Australia.

Astrolabe An astronomical instrument used for measuring the angles of stars or the sun (*right*). By looking up the angle in a set of tables, navigators could work out their latitude.

Bathyscape A submersible vessel with an airtight flotation compartment and an observation capsule.

Cannibal People that eat the flesh of their own kind.

Caravan In Asia or Africa, a group of merchants traveling together with pack animals.

Caravel A light, fast vessel of the 15th century with a mixture of square and triangular sails.

Cartography The technical term for mapmaking.

Chronometer A very accurate clock used for working out longitude at sea (*right*).

Compass A device used to indicate north. The first compasses were pieces of lodestone (naturally magnetic rock). These were later replaced by magnetized steel needles.

Conquistador A conqueror, usually one of the conquerors of Mexico and Peru.

Dhow Arabian lateen-rigged ships (*right*).

El Dorado The fabled city of gold believed by explorers to exist in South America.

Glacier A mass of ice that moves downhill under the force of gravity.

Iceberg A huge lump of ice that has detached itself from the end of a glacier.

Ice Floe A small iceberg (*left*).

Imperialism The policy of building an empire.

Junk A Chinese sailing vessel of ancient origin. It has a flat bottom with a large rudder instead of a keel.

Latitude The distance of a point on the Earth's surface north or south of the equator, measured in degrees.

Longitude The distance of a point on the Earth's surface east or west of the half circle that runs from the North to the South Pole through Greenwich, London.

Magnetic Pole The place on the Earth's surface to which all compass needles point. This point is not fixed, and is currently in the far north of Canada.

Mermaids The half-women, half-fish of legend that may have been dugongs, a type of marine mammal (*above*)!

Missionary Someone sent out to spread a religious message.

Mutiny A revolt against authority.

Navigation Finding your way.

New World The European term for America after its discovery.

Pillars of Hercules The Straits of Gibraltar, where the Atlantic Ocean meets the Mediterranean Sea.

Rig The arrangement of a ship's masts and sails.

Satellite Man-made carriers of instruments placed in orbit around the Earth.

Sextant A navigational instrument used for measuring the angle of the stars or sun.

Square Rig A rig with square sails set at right angles to their mast.

Submersible A vessel that can operate underwater.

Triangular (or lateen) rig A rig with triangular sails hoisted to the top of (usually short) masts (*above*).

Whirlpool A circular current in the sea produced by opposing tides or winds.

EXPLORERS' TIMELINE

40,000 B.C. *Homo sapiens* colonizes the world as the great Ice Age ends.

c.2300 B.C. Harkhuf explores the upper Nile.

334 B.C. Alexander the Great invades Asia, reaching India in 329 B.C.

308 B.C. Pytheas of Marseilles sails north to England and possibly Norway.

c. 150 A.D. Ptolemy draws his famous atlas *Geography*.

3rd century A.D. The Chinese develop the magnetic compass.

6th century A.D. St. Brendan's voyage across the Atlantic Ocean.

750 Settlement of New Zealand by Polynesians (*above*).

c. 1000 Vikings settle in Greenland and Vinland.

1154 Publication of Al-Idrisi's giant atlas *Book of Roger*.

1275 Marco Polo arrives in China.

1325–1349 Travels of Ibn Battuta to Africa and Asia.

1404–1433 In seven voyages, Cheng Ho visits 30 countries around the Indian Ocean (*right*).

1434–1460 Portuguese King Henry the Navigator sponsors voyages along the African coast.

1492–1493 Christopher Columbus's (*below left*) first Atlantic voyage.

1497 John Cabot reaches Newfoundland.

1498 Vasco da Gama arrives in India.

1522 Magellan's expedition, led by del Cano, completes the first voyage around the globe.

1518-1522 Hernán Cortés conquers the Aztecs.

1531–1535 Francisco Pizarro conquers the Incas.

1542 Francisco de Orellana sails down the Amazon.

1611 Henry Hudson dies trying to find the Northwest Passage to Asia.

1682 Robert de la Salle journeys down the Mississippi River.

1719 Daniel Defoe writes *Robinson Crusoe*.

1726 Jonathan Swift writes his classic story *Gulliver's Travels*.

1768–1779 Captain James Cook charts large areas of the South Pacific, including Tahiti, New Zealand, and Australia.

1796 Mungo Park reaches the Niger River.

1798 Samuel Coleridge writes his great poem, *The Rime of the Ancient Mariner*.

1804–1806 Lewis & Clark (*below*) lead an expedition from St. Louis to the Pacific.

1851 Herman Melville writes *Moby Dick*.

1853–1856 David Livingstone crosses Africa.

1858 John Speke discovers Lake Victoria.

1860–1861 Burke & Wills lead an expedition across Australia from south to north.

1867–1877 Przewalski makes five expeditions into Central Asia.

1876–1877 Stanley travels down the Congo to Africa.

1885 Henry Rider Haggard writes *King Solomon's Mines*.

1911 Roald Amundsen wins the race to the South Pole. His rival Robert Scott reaches the Pole a month later.

1922 Alexandra David-Neale becomes the first European woman to enter Lhasa.

1930 Amy Johnson is the first woman to fly solo from England to Australia.

1953 Tenzing Norgay and Sir Edmund Hillary climb Mount Everest.

1960 Jacques Piccard sinks to the deepest point in the ocean in the *Trieste*.

1969 Neil Armstrong walks on the moon.

2020 The first manned mission to Mars (*right*)?

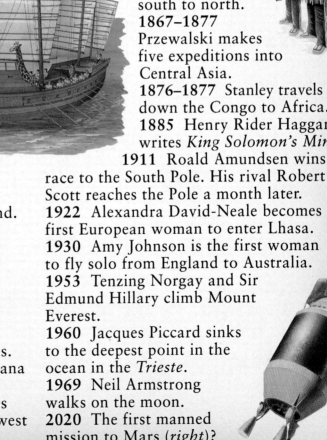

INDEX

Photo credits *Abbreviations: t – top, m – middle, b – bottom, l – left, r – right.*

Cover, 4-5, 9t, 14 both, 19m, 20b, 21t, 22b, 23t, 27t, 28t, 29t, 33t, 34m, 36m – Mary Evans Picture Library; 6t, 15, 18, 26, 29b, 30, 34t, 35t, 37b, 38b, 43b, 45b – Frank Spooner Pictures; 6b, 12, 20 –21, 43, 45m – Ronald Grant Archive; 7 both, 11t, 20t, 32t – AKG London; 8t, 9b, 10, 17t, 19b, 23b, 33m, 35m, 40, 41b, 44m – Kobal Collection; 11b – Ancient Art & Architecture Collection; 13b, 25t – Eye Ubiquitous; 17m – Solution Pictures; 22t, 29m – Roger Vlitos; 27m, 36t – Hutchison Library; 31 – Bruce Coleman Collection; 36b, 38t, 39, 41t, 42 – Hulton Getty Collection; 44t & b – NASA.